Talking About Time

Days of the Week

Jilly Attwood

Raintree

Chicago, Illinois

© 2005 Raintree
Published by Raintree, a division of Reed Elsevier, Inc.
Chicago, Illinois
Customer Service 888-363-4266
Visit our website at www.raintreelibrary.com

Printed and bound by South China Printing Company.
09 08 07 06 05
10 9 8 7 6 5 4 3 2 1

Library of Congress Cataloging-in-Publication Data:
Attwood, Jilly.
  Talking about time : days of the week / Jilly Attwood.
    p. cm.
  ISBN 1-4109-1638-3 (library binding-hardcover) -- ISBN 1-4109-1644-8 (pbk.) 1. Day--Juvenile literature. 2. Week--Juvenile literature. I. Title.
  CE85.A88 2005
  529'.1--dc22

                              2004025558

Acknowledgments
The publishers would like to thank the following for permission to reproduce photographs: Alamy p. 15; Corbis pp. 11, 17; Digital vision p. 19 (Rob Van Petten); Getty images/Photodisc p. 17b; Harcourt Education pp. 12, 16, 21a (Trevor Clifford), 13, 14, 17a (Gareth Boden); Tudor Photography pp. 9, 10, 18, 20, 21b.

Cover photograph reproduced with permission of Corbis (Ariel Skelley).

Some words are shown in *bold*, **like this**. You can find out what they mean by looking in the glossary on page 24.

Contents

Days of the Week

There are seven days of the **week**.

FEBRUARY

MON	TUE	WED	THUR	FRI	SAT	SUN
			1	2	3	4
5	6	7	8	9	10	11
12	13	14	15	16	17	18
19	20	21	22	23	24	25
26	27	28				

○ FULL MOON (8)

NEW MOON (23)

JANUARY

M	1	8	15	22	29
T	2	9	16	23	30
W	3	10	17	24	31
T	4	11	18	25	
F	5	12	19	26	
S	6	13	20	27	
S	7	14	21	28	

MARCH

M		5	12	19	26
T		6	13	20	27
W		7	14	21	28
T	1	8	15	22	29
F	2	9	16	23	30
S	3	10	17	24	31
S	4	11	18	25	

New Year's Day	1 January
Bank Holiday (Scotland)	2 January
Bank Holiday (N. Ireland)	19 March
Good Friday	13 April
Easter Monday (holiday - except Scotland)	16 April
Bank Holiday	7 May
Bank Holiday	28 May
Bank Holiday (N. Ireland)	12 July
Bank Holiday (Scotland)	6 August
Bank Holiday (except Scotland)	27 August
Christmas Day	25 December
Boxing Day	26 December

SEE BACK OF DECEMBER ... OR COMPLETE CALENDAR

Do you know what they are called?

5

It's Monday

Annie goes to **school**. Her dad goes to work. Do you go to school?

It's Tuesday

It's library time.

The children choose a book to take home.

It's macaroni and cheese for lunch today!

Yummy!

It's Wednesday

This morning Mrs. Rashid shows the class how to roll dough.

roll

roll

splash

Joe and Matthew go swimming after school.

It's Thursday

Today the dentist
is shows the class
how to use a toothbrush.

Do you know how to
brush your teeth?

Sparkle

In the **afternoon** it's music time.

Do you like to make music?

Today the class makes clay dinosaurs.

ROAR!

14

15

It's Saturday

Kelly and her mom go shopping on Saturday.

What do you like to do on Saturday?

17

It's Sunday

Sam helps his mom wash the car.

scrub

scrub

Keisha has a big lunch with her family.

Special days

Some days are special days.

Seven days

Tuesday

Monday

Sunday

Wednesday

Thursday

Friday

Saturday

23

Glossary

afternoon   the part of the day after 12.00 P.M.
school   a place to learn
week   seven days in a row

Index

Notes for adults

The *Talking about time* series introduces young children to the concept of time. By relating their own experiences to specific moments in time, the children can start to explore the pattern of regular events that occur in a day, week or year.

This book focuses on the seven days of the week and shows what children might do on each day of the week, at school and at home. The book provides an opportunity for children to discuss and compare their own daily activities. The use of the word *time*, such as in *library time*, helps to reinforce how some activities happen over a set period of time. The book also introduces the concept of special days such as birthdays and holidays.

Follow-up activity
Make a mural of pictures and photos to show the different activities the children do on each day of the week. Keep a picture journal for a week to record what the child has done each day.